CW00551067

COMPING STANDA

for

JAZZ GUITAR

Jim Ferguson

1 2

Visit us on the Web at www.melbay.com — E-mail us at email@melbay.com

Published by:
Guitar Master Class
www.fergusonguitar.com

Other publications By Jim Ferguson:

- *All Blues For Jazz Guitar—Comping Styles, Chords & Grooves*
- *All Blues Soloing For Jazz Guitar—Scales, Licks, Concepts & Choruses*
- *All Blues Scale For Jazz Guitar—Solos, Grooves & Patterns*
- *All Solos & Grooves For Jazz Guitar—Position Studies, Scales & Patterns*
- *All Intros & Endings For Jazz Guitar—Bebop, Swing, Latin, Ballads*
- *Shapes, Patterns & Lines For Jazz Guitar*

Exclusively distributed by Mel Bay Publications, Inc.

Proofing and photo (page 32) courtesy of Diane Haggerty
Graphics and layout by GMCP

CONTENTS

INTRODUCTION & PRELIMINARY TIPS

My book *All Blues For Jazz Guitar—Comping Styles, Chords & Grooves* covers comping in a blues context. *Comping Standards* builds on that theme by addressing standard tunes. Although it is hoped that you eventually look at this material from start to finish so you have a more complete understanding of the topic at hand, feel free to begin at any point. Also, I suggest that you use this book in conjunction with not only *All Blues for Jazz Guitar*, but also my *All Intros & Endings For Jazz Guitar—Bebop, Swing, Latin, Ballads*, the content of which is directly applicable to that of this book.

To make this material as easy to apply as possible, most of the common jazz keys are represented here, including G, C, F, Bb, Eb, and Ab major, and C and E minor. As you work your way through this book and apply its approaches to real playing situations, the following points are good to keep in mind:

Keep your volume below that of the soloist. When you are comping, you are playing a supporting role, which means that you can't overwhelm the soloist. In other words, don't play too loud.

Improvisation. Despite playing a supporting role, remember that you, too, are improvising. Of course, the degree to which you improvise depends on the type of rhythmic role you are playing. For instance, if you are in a situation that calls for a straight-four approach with three-note voicings on strings three, four, and six, your options for variety will be limited. Still, variation is possible. So if you find yourself playing the same exact chords over and over again, make it a goal to expand your chordal and rhythmic vocabularies. That being said, during a tune's head, the chords you choose can't clash with the melody.

Fingerings. It's highly advantageous to be able to finger a chord in more than one way. Also, when changing from chord to chord, only lift your fingers off of a string if it is absolutely necessary. When you keep a finger on a string as you move from fret to fret, it is called a "guide." When a finger remains on the same string at the same fret as you change chords, it is called a "pivot." While not always possible, guides and pivots, concepts borrowed from classical guitar technique, can dramatically increase your fingering efficiency and mean the difference between smooth or choppy playing. Throughout this book, guides are indicated with a dash before the fingering number.

Chord equivalents & the b5 substitute. Also known as chord synonyms, equivalents are one of the most basic aspects of hip chord usage. The following list shows some of the most common chord equivalents, ones that are used throughout this book:

Cmaj7 = Am9 (no root)

C6 = Am7 = Fmaj9 (no root)

Cdim7 = B7b9 (no root)

Cm7b5 = Ab9 (no root) = Ebm6 = D7#5b9 (no root)

C9b5 (no root) = Gb7#5

Observe that C9b5 = Gb7#5 (often spelled as F#7#5), shown in the last line of the preceding list, is the often-discussed b5 relationship. Any dominant chord can be used in this manner, although the result may not be an exact equivalent. Not only does the b5 substitute generate altered chordal tones, but also it frequently approaches the next chord from a half-step above, as in the sequence Db13-Cm7, where Db13 is a b5 substitute for G7, the V7 of Cm7. (Additional note: Since the 9th of IIIm7 is lowered, avoid its use in most cases.)

Here are some of the preceding equivalents seen in context. Separately they are complete structures (Fmaj7, Fm7b5, and Em7); however, when used to create a IIm7-V7-I in C, they are all rootless:

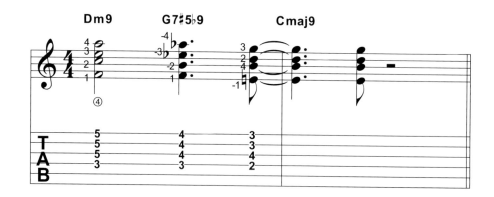

Since rootless chords at first can be difficult to locate on the fretboard, you can make the process more manageable by visualizing a nearby root, which then serves as a "locator." While an imaginary bass locator is probably most convenient, you may prefer a different option. The diagram opposite shows a rootless B♭9 chord (A♭, C, D, low to high), with potential locators on the sixth, third, and first strings.

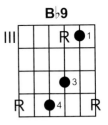

Partial chords. While rootless chords are partial chords, they also fall into a class of harmonies know as chord fragments or chords of omission. Partial chords enable you to cover a vast harmonic landscape and exercise a great deal of control over the music's texture and harmonic connections. It is most common to omit a chord's 5th and root; however, partial chords can omit the 7th and even the 3rd. While a comprehensive discussion of partial (including rootless) chords is beyond the scope of this book, the following example shows an easy way to generate partial structures from a single common chord, in this case Cmaj9, where playing certain string combinations results in a series of partial structures. The last part of the example shows the 3rd and the 7th, the so-called guide tones:

Cmaj9   Cmaj7   Cmaj9   Cmaj7

Playing with a pianist can be one of the most challenging aspects of being a rhythm player, because the guitar is usually in a subordinate role. Minimize clutter by staying out of the pianist's way. This can be done in any number of manners, including not playing at all. When the piano part is busy, try playing simply, using not overly embellished chords and a predictable rhythmic pattern. Try to operate in a range that the pianist isn't covering. Sometimes, playing something as simple as only guide tones can work. Then there's the act of "sprinkling," which is similar to filling in the rhythmic/melodic holes. With sprinkling, you are playing very sparsely and often in a high register.

Basic/realized. Notice these designations at the beginning of each song example. The "basic" row refers to how the chord changes might appear in a fake book, whereas the "realized" row shows how the chart might be interpreted in a real playing situation. Fake-book charts generally need little or no reharmonization, since they often are either created by a jazz composer in the first place or are a transcription of a notable performance by an experienced, well-known musician.

Tempo & Rhythm. The most important aspect of rhythm is holding a tempo, whether it be fast or slow, while maintaining a feel that is appropriate to the music. (The tempo indications at the beginning of each piece should serve as a general guide only.) The use of off-the-beat rhythmic figures can be very hip, especially when they anticipate a new chord change, and can be found in most sections of this book. Being able to add a punctuation or begin a phrase on any part of any beat (within reason) can be a powerful resource. If the chords and rhythms are too much to handle at first, feel free to simplify the rhythms to whole-, half-, and quarter-notes. There are many other rhythmic figures than the ones shown here; use these examples as a foundation on which to build your own ideas.

Form is the overall structure of a tune. In jazz, there are several common configurations consisting of 12, 32, and 64 measures. The 32-bar form usually can be broken down into either two 16-bar sections or four 8-bar sections and can be described as A^1A^2 (where the second 16 ends differently from the first 16) or AABA (the B section is often referred to as the "bridge"), respectively.

Finally, keep in mind that in certain ensemble settings, it's possible to use all three of the basic approaches described in this book, sometimes simultaneously. For instance, if you are playing with another guitarist, you might use moving bass lines at one point, smoothly transition to a straight-four approach, and even incorporate combo-style comping. Exactly how you might do this is up to your own taste and command of the material. I also highly recommend that you play each of the pieces featured here with all three approaches. To help you do that, I've presented "Into Somewhere" in straight-four, walking bass, and combo-comping contexts.

Jim Ferguson
Santa Cruz, California, 2014

1 STRAIGHT-FOUR—COMPING WITH THREE-NOTE FAT CHORDS

The following three-note open-voiced chords, used extensively by figures such as Freddie Green, Herb Ellis, Jim Hall, and George Barnes (who coined the term "fat chords"), are highly versatile. They work great in a big band setting, and can also lead to advanced fingerboard knowledge, arranging, and even composition.

These chords are satisfying for two reasons. First, the interval from the lowest to the highest note is a tenth, a very pleasing sound. Second, since they are usually played for this type of approach on strings six, four, and three, they enable you to make smooth connections from chord to chord, where the notes often move by step. Be sure to damp the fifth string with a finger of your left hand (usually the index), and control your right-hand stroke so that it stops short of the second string. The damped string is part of the percussive aspect of this approach.

While a complete discussion of chord voicings and inversions is beyond the scope of this book, it's good to know that when a three-note voicing based on a 7th chord is systematically inverted, each resulting structure omits one of the four tones, illustrated by the following example:

"**Into Somewhere**" uses a 16-bar form repeated twice; the overall treatment is straightforward.

In measure 1, the symbols above the staff indicate down pick strokes, while the ones between the standard and tab staffs are articulations; the upper set has a more uniform sound, while the lower one, which emphasizes beats 2 and 4, is a bit more bouncy. In bar 2, a first-inversion G triad is used to smooth the transition from Gmaj7 to B♭m7. And notice that from measure 17 to the beginning of bar 20, the chords descend smoothly. The last two bars of the second ending include a I-VI-II-V progression that turns things back to the top.

A repeat is used for space considerations. In a real playing situation, try to avoid playing repetitions in the same exact way.

"Into Somewhere"

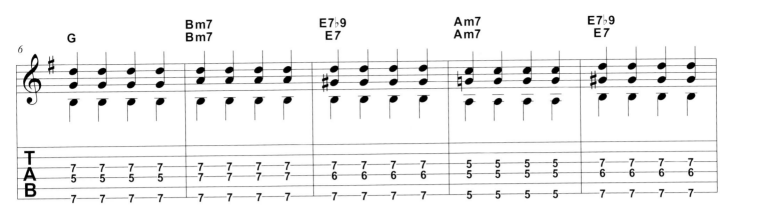

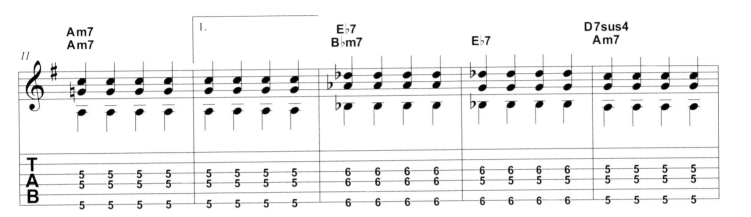

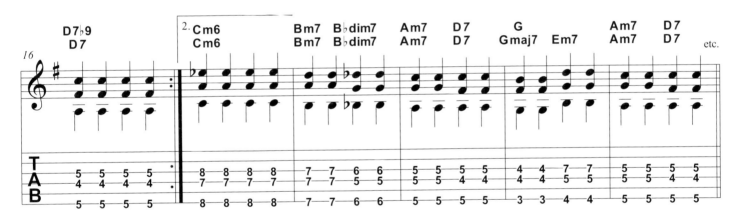

"**We Can't Be Parted**" is a 32-bar ballad in the key of C major. The bridge begins on IIIm7, which functions as IIm7, signalling a temporary key change to D major. Again, repeats save space.

One difference between this tune and "Into Somewhere" is the use of passing chords. In bar 2, a rootless F7 (also the equivalent of Cm6 and Cdim7) is used to connect G7 to Bm7, and C6 to Em7 in measures 11 and 12. Diminished 7th chords particularly work well in passing and can approach another chord from either a half-step above or below, as well as chromatically connect the bass notes of two chords a whole-step apart. Again, remember that a three-note voicing based on a 7th chord omits a note, depending on the structure of the starting point (root-position chord). Subsequent systematic inversions in turn omit one of the remaining three chordal tones. Also, experiment with approaching each chord from a half-step above or below. For instance, bar 1 could be played Cmaj7-Bb7-A7-Eb7.

Bars 3, 4, 13, and 17 depart from the strict straight-four feel with a sixteenth-note figure on beats 1 or 3, which adds a bit of punch to the part. Used with discretion, rhythmic departures can be very effective, and you can also occasionally interject higher-voiced chords. The idea of mixing voicings is discussed in Chapter 5, although in a different context.

To repeat the entire 32-bar structure, take the first ending after the D.C., and then begin again at bar 1. To end the tune, take the second ending and then the coda, a brief ending featuring a half-step approach to the tonic chord.

Track 2

"We Can't Be Parted"

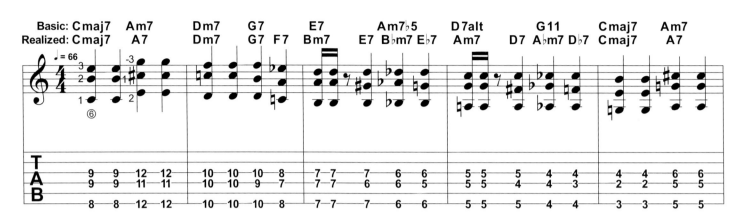

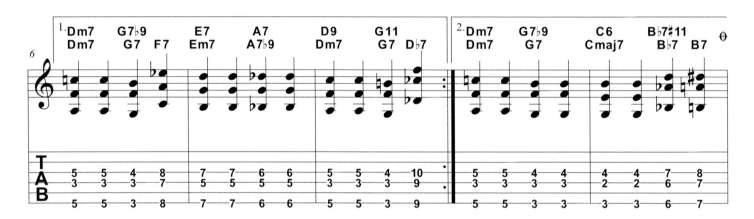

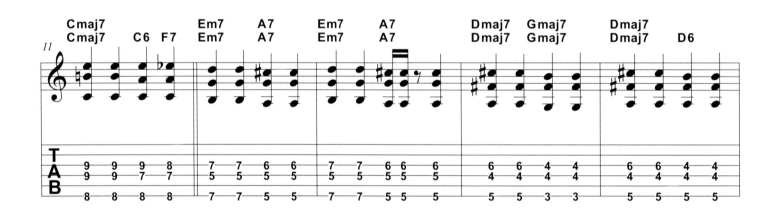

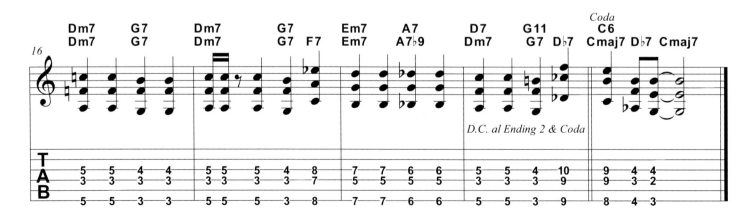

2 MOVING BASS LINES—SWING & LATIN

As Joe Pass demonstrated throughout his illustrious career, the art of moving bass lines is one of the hippest comping approaches, especially when playing in an ensemble setting where the guitar is the primary harmonic instrument. The examples in this section feature three complete tunes, including one we've seen before and a Latin example. (While "moving" includes walking lines, it also encompasses Latin bass movements.)

The following pieces will give your left-hand a real workout. To make things easier, carefully follow the fingerings, using guides whenever possible. At first, practice slowly until you can bring things up to the indicated tempo. And remember: The bass line is the most important part of this approach.

Bass lines commonly move in the following ways: by scale step, chromatically, by skip (often based on chordal tones), and by root-5th motion. All of these are used in the following examples. Also try to vary your rhythmic treatment of the chords, sometimes playing them on the beat, and sometimes off, which will relieve the monotony of playing the chords in only one way.

"**Into Somewhere**" is back again with a more elaborate treatment.

In measure 1, the G bass leaps down to E before moving up chromatically. The first three beats of bar 3 move by scale step, while root-5th movement is used in measures 8, 12, 14, 16, and 17. Also, it's possible to rhythmically vary the bass line, illustrated in bars 12 and 16.

Finally, notice the occasional use of open strings (bars 8 and 16), which, among other things, facilitate a position change.

Track 3

"Into Somewhere"

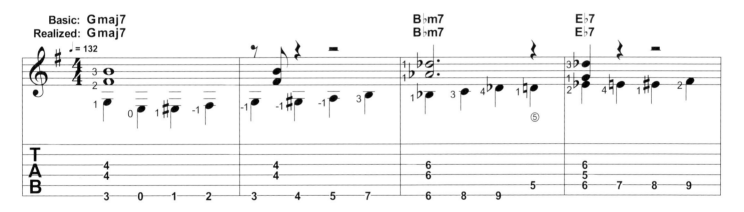

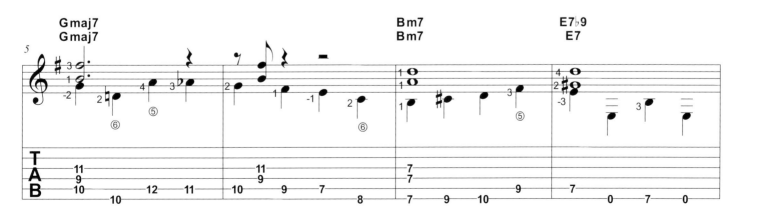

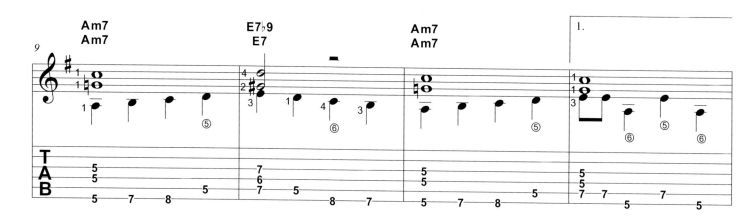

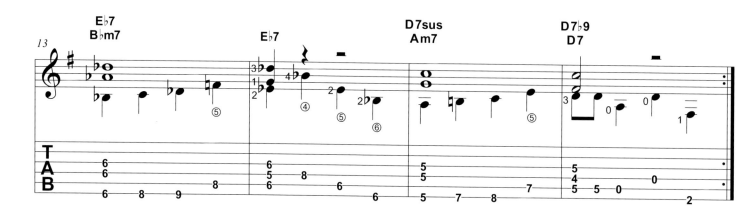

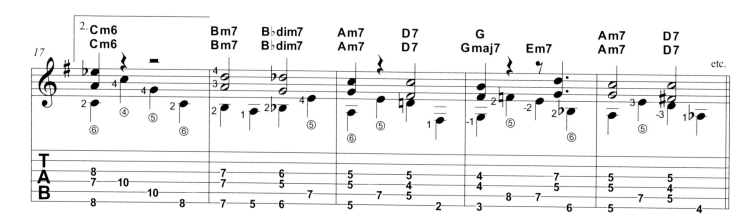

"**Rhythm Changes**." Variations of this 32-bar progression are used for several jazz standards, including "I Got Rhythm," "Thriving On A Riff," "Rhythm-a-ning," and "Cottontail." Again, all of the basic bass movements are employed: step, chromatic, and leap (including root-5th). To take the coda, you can either repeat from the top as instructed or take it the first time through.

The root of any chord can be approached from a half- or scale-step above or below, as shown in bars 1 through 3. In bars 3 and 4, ♭5 substitutes vary the monotony of the usual progression and also offer a different set of options for the bass line.

A long series of root-5th relationships is used from measures 5 through 8, while an episode of straight-four appears in bar 11 through the first half of 12.

The bridge, beginning in measure 17, is very common in both its basic and realized versions. The former (which "back cycles" through the circle of fifths) is generally considered to be old style, while the latter is an updated version that turns the basic chords into a series of IIm7-V7s.

Finally, notice the rit. indication in the coda, which signals a gradual slowing until the final chord.

"Rhythm Changes"

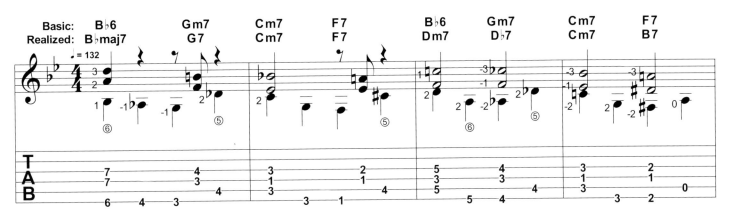

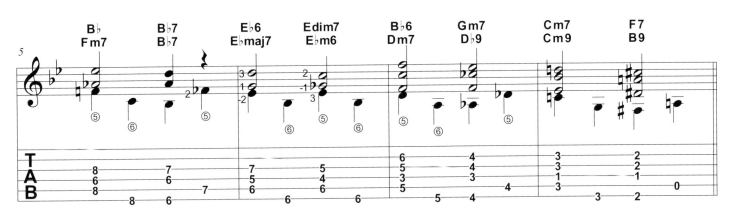

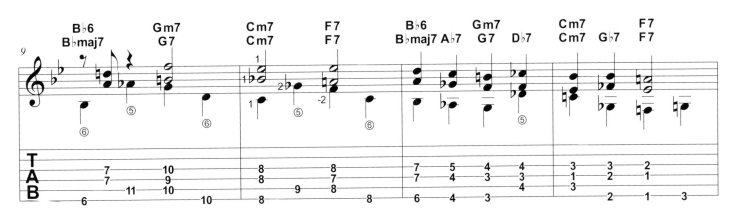

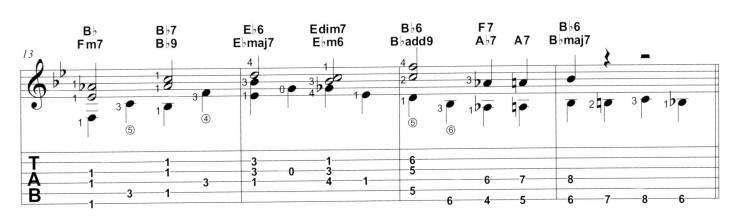

Comping Standards

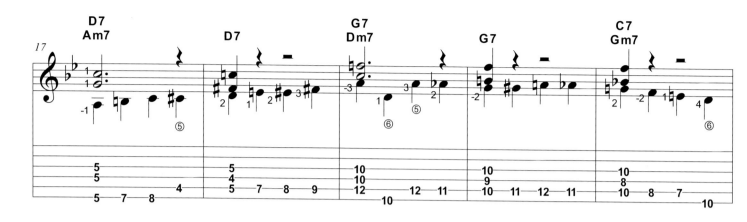

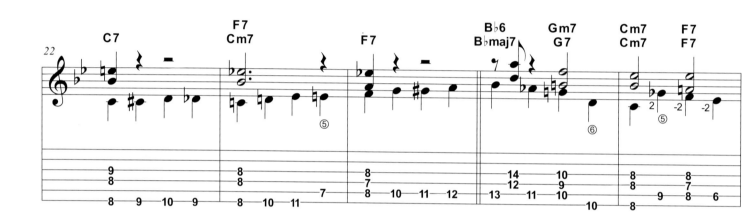

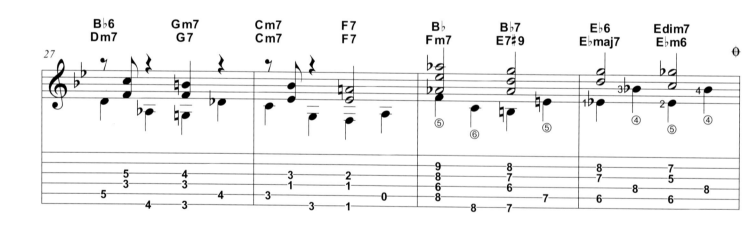

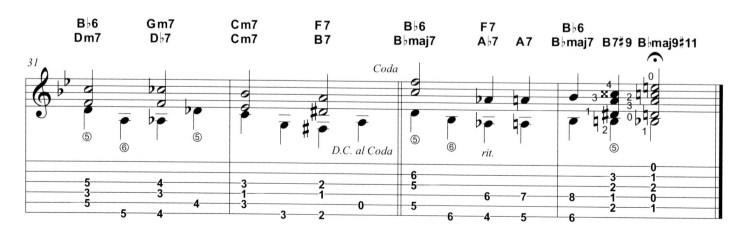

"**Deep Blue Bossa**" is a 16-bar tune that demonstrates how a moving bass can be applied to Brazilian tunes. Here, notice how the bass moves in increments of two beats. Root-5th movement is featured throughout. To include an opening vamp and an extended ending, use the same rhythmic scheme with the chords Cm9-Db9.

A bossa nova usually can accommodate several rhythmic patterns. The one used here anticipates the chord of the next measure, a common feature of Brazilian music. (Because of this anticipation, it's sometimes necessary to cut short the second bass note by an eighth value.)

"Deep Blue Bossa"

3 COMBO COMPING WITH OPEN-VOICED THREE-NOTE CHORDS

Open-voiced three-note chords can be used in more ways than for straight-four or walking bass lines. When moved to strings five, three, and two (they can even be moved up to the next string set), they work great in a combo setting.

Although conservative in nature due both to their characteristic tenth interval between the outer notes and the fact that you'll often be redundantly playing the root along with the bassist, their voiceleading potential enables you to function almost as if you were a mini horn section.

"Confirmation Blues." Known by several names, including "New York Blues" and "II-V Blues," this 12-bar progression is rife with IIm7-V7s. Learn the rhythmic figures well, and then feel free to experiment with not only the ideas presented here, but also your own.

In measure 1, a "fall" is indicated. Play the chord, and then gliss down until the sound dies away. And check out the chromatic minor chords in bars 3 and 4, a device that works well in many other tunes. Bars 6 through 10 feature a series of chromatic IIm7-V7s, while the turnaround in measures 11 and 12 is one associated with Wes Montgomery, although he invariably used root-position chords.

"Confirmation Blues"

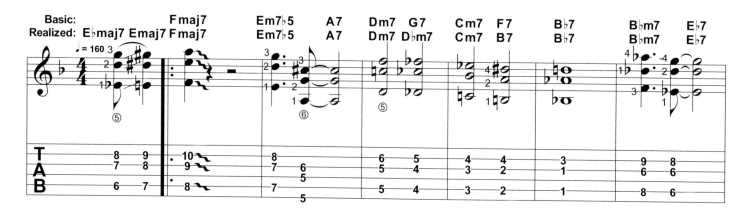

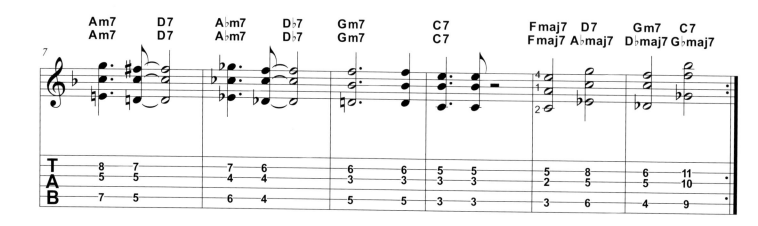

"Always Autumn." This 32-bar tune is in the key of E minor (but starts with IV minor), a relative rarity in terms of jazz standards, which tend to favor major keys.

As in "Confirmation Blues," second inversion resolves to root position (bars 1 through 6 and 16 through 19). And chromatic minor chords are featured in measures 8, 15, and 22 and 23.

Two chords are of special interest: In bars 6, 13, 21, and 25, Badd9 (the equivalent of D♯m7) is used to connect B7 to Em7. And measures 10, 11, 26, and 27 feature a thirdless third-inversion Em7. As noted before, a three-note 7th chord must omit one of its notes, and in third inversion that note will be the 3rd. Without its 3rd, a chord sounds ambiguous, an effect that should be used sparingly but at the same time can produce cool results.

Throughout, similar rhythmic figures are used that frequently anticipate a chord change. Learn these rhythms well and they will serve you well.

"Always Autumn"

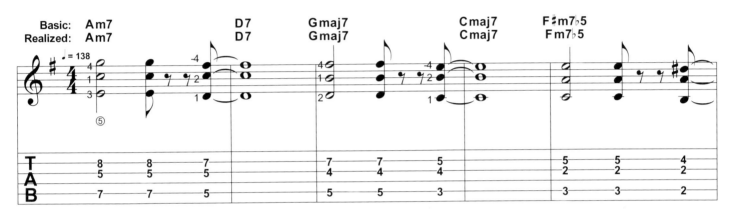

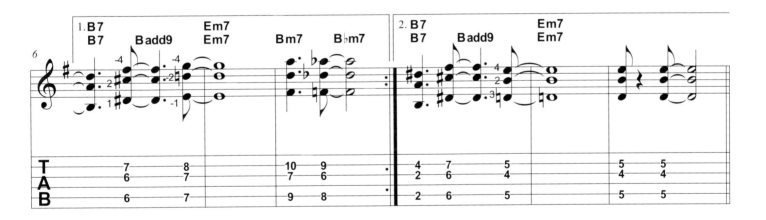

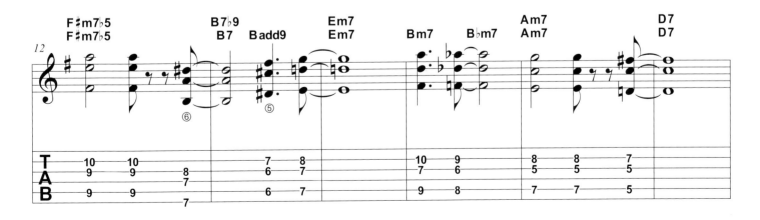

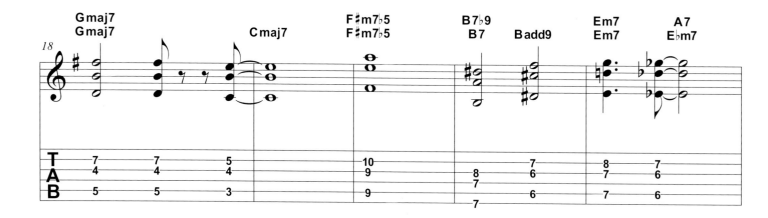

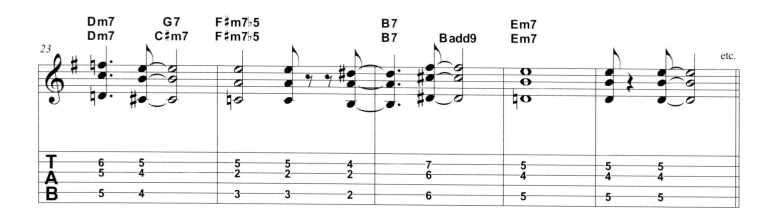

"**Un Peu Blues**." This book's only tune in 3/4, "Un Peu Blues" is in the key of B♭ major and uses only three rhythmic patterns (see bars 1, 3, and 5).

As mentioned in the Introduction, you should be able to finger a chord in more than one manner. The fingering in measure 1 enables you to use the 4th finger as a guide to the chords in bars 2 and 3. (The use of a first-inversion B♭ major chord in measure 2 helps connect B♭maj7 to Am7♭5.)

Notice the pick direction indications in bar 5. When strumming in this manner, be sure to sound all of the notes in the chord while muting (or not sounding) strings that aren't included. Muting can be accomplished by touching a string with a part of a left-hand finger.

This piece is rife with IIm7-V7s, as in bars 3 and 4, 5 and 6, 7 and 8, 11 and 12, 15 and 16, and 19 and 20.

Finally, the C♭7 in measure 24 is a ♭5 substitute that continues the chromatic descent that begins in bar 21.

"Un Peu Blues"

Track 8

4 COMBO COMPING— 7th CHORDS & BEYOND

While 7th chords are a necessary part of the jazz harmonic vocabulary, the hippest sounds are generated by including extensions (the 9th, 11th, and 13th) and/or alterations (♯5, ♭5/♯11, ♭9, and ♯9), which is often accomplished by using chord equivalents.

More active comping. Effective comping is more than just playing the right chords. In order to react to what the other band members are doing and to make your playing more kinetic, you need a larger chordal vocabulary. While a comprehensive discussion of guitar harmony is beyond the scope of this book, the following will both expand and help organize your chordal knowledge.

Chord scales. Developing a comprehensive command of jazz-related harmonies on the guitar can be an arduous task. While certain open-voiced 7th chords can be systematically inverted and then manipulated to generate other chord qualities, many jazz guitar harmonies defy systemization because they are frequently incomplete structures for which there is no common procedure and nomenclature and are bound by the instrument's tuning and resulting fingerboard complexities.

Chord scales provide a powerful way to organize chords on the guitar's fingerboard. The following examples show the F major scale, the C chromatic scale, and the G Dorian mode harmonized with 4-note chords (the scale itself is carried by the uppermost note of each chord on the first string). (Observe that here, each chord is either an F major-, C dominant-, or G minor-type chord. This type of chord scale differs from that of the harmonized scale, where each note moves up by step to a chord with a different root.)

To initially simplify the learning process, the same chord form is used whenever possible, although each scale step can be harmonized with more than one voicing. Once you learn the chords given, continue to expand your harmonic vocabulary as you discover other possibilities.

A few words on the chord scales themselves: The "weak" tone of the F major scale is its 4th note; the corresponding chord should be used only in passing. Regarding the harmonized chromatic scale, notice the absence of the major 7th degree (B), which, apart from exceptional situations, is incompatible with dominant harmonies. The Dorian mode is straightforward (observe the first and last chords, which show two different voicings that support the note F). Practice these scales both ascending and descending, and then work on assembling some IIm (Dorian)-V7 (chromatic)-Imaj combinations by moving from a chord or chords in the third line (Dorian) to the second line (chromatic) to the first line.

Eventually, you'll want to learn chord scales whose upper note is on the second and even third string. More on this coming up.

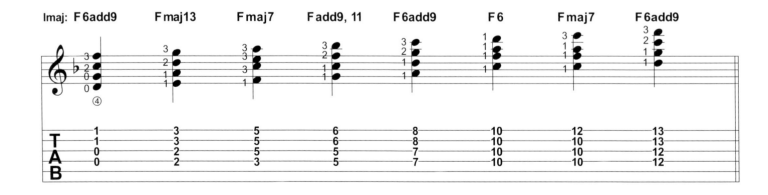

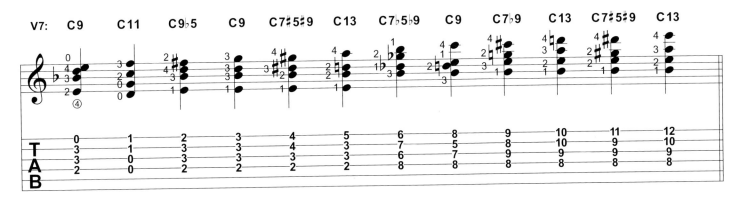

Again, it's important to know that each note of the preceding scales can be harmonized with more than one voicing. For instance, the following example shows the second note of the F major scale (G) harmonized in five additional ways (in this case there are even more possibilities). Try using each of these for the second scale tone (G) of the preceding F major scale. As you learn more chords, fit them into the appropriate chord scale and think of them as available alternatives to the voicings presented here.

Once you've developed some fluency moving from chord to chord in the preceding scales, for practice purposes you can thread them into IIm7-V7-Imaj7 sequences. The following example shows two possibilities; in bars 1 and 2 of each example, two versions of the same chord are used (the second example connects chords with single notes, an approach that can be used in comping):

"**Gnawing On The Apple.**" Now let's apply chord scales to this uptempo number in the key of Fmajor, although it starts on IIm (here, IIm9).

This rhythmically and harmonically active comp often employs chords that not only move frequently—especially during the bridge—but are often extended and rootless due to the use of equivalents. The result frequently is a melody formed by the uppermost note of each chord, which can enable you to complement and interact with the soloist and/or rhythm section. At points, chords not in the previously presented chord scales are introduced. Be sure to match them up with the corresponding chord scale.

The second chord in bar 8 is particularly hip and is equivalent to A♭13.

Measure 11 features a device that you'll also find in some of the tunes coming up: The delayed resolution, where Gm9 in bar 11 continues into the first half of bar 12, leads to C7♯5♯9 and then to Fmaj7. Notice the syncopations in measures 1, 3, 9, 11, and 27, which both provide a break from playing so many chords and help propel the tune.

Another aspect of this comp is that in places, it doesn't actualize all of the chords (see bars 7, 15, 31, and 32), a perfectly acceptable practice, especially with uptempo numbers.

"Gnawing On The Apple"

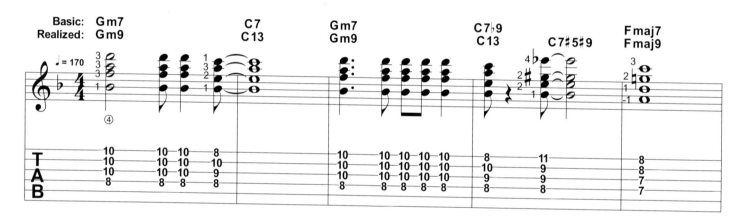

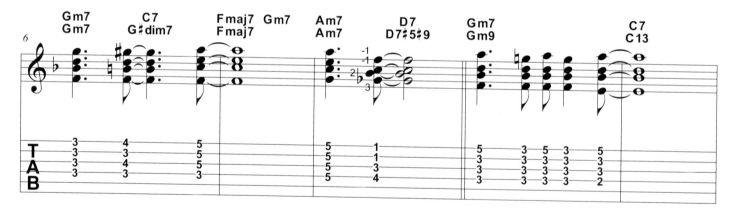

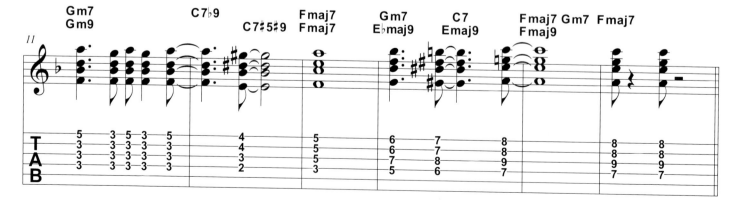

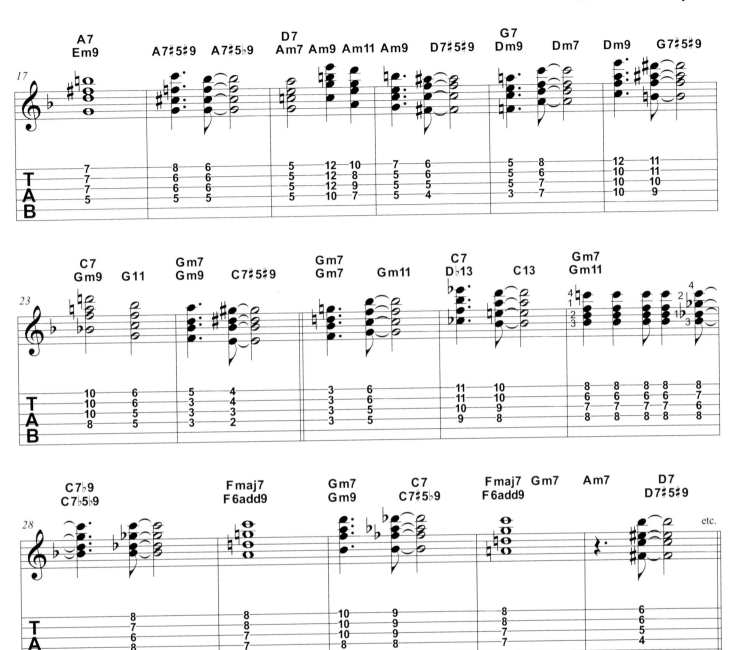

"**Minor Blues**." This active minor blues comp frequently uses extended and rootless voicings from the previously presented chord scales, along with a m7♭5 voicing in bars 9, 10, and 12.

It's good to keep in mind that there is more than one way to achieve more active chordal movement, one of which would be to take a modal approach; for Cm7, this could result in Cm7-Dm7♭5-E♭maj7-Dm7♭5-Cm7, keeping in mind that the prevailing mode is C Aeolian (more on this later). Here a more direct method is used via a series of harmonies whose roots, even though often not present in the chords themselves, match that of the chord at hand. The only exceptions to this occur in measures 4, 6, and 11, where a dominant chord resolves to a minor chord a half-step down. (This device is similar to a simple half-step approach, but can produce a hipper result.)

Again, the prevailing mode is Aeolian, which differs from Dorian in that it has a lowered 6th degree (in this case, A♭). Since the 6th is included in only one member of the Dorian chord scale presented on page 19, you can freely draw upon the remaining voicings and avoid committing a modal conflict that results in a clash of tonalities.

The tune begins with Cm9 in bar 1 into bar 2 and then begins to transition to IV minor via chord scale members before it moves to G♭13, a ♭5 substitute for C7, the V7 of IVm7 (measure 4). The same device of using a dominant to resolve to a minor chord is used in bar 6, where D♭13 (the ♭5 substitute of G7) returns to Cm9.

The remainder of the tune features one chord per change, where two different chromatic series lead to Cm9, the first in bars 9 and 10, and the second in bars 11 and 12, the turnaround.

"Minor Blues"

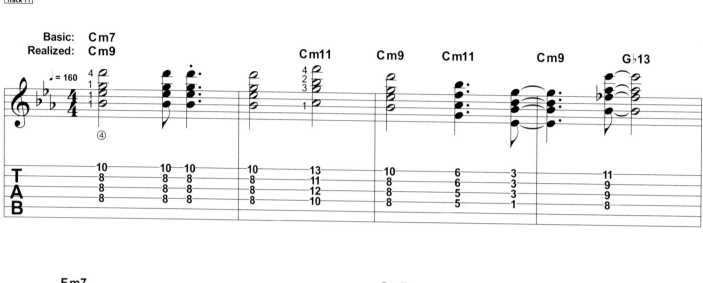

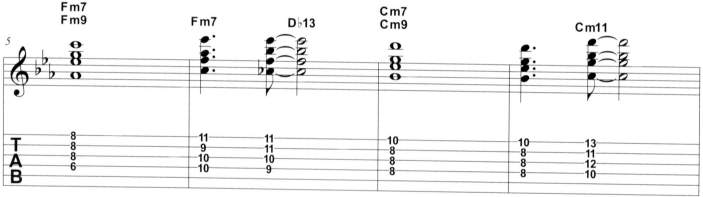

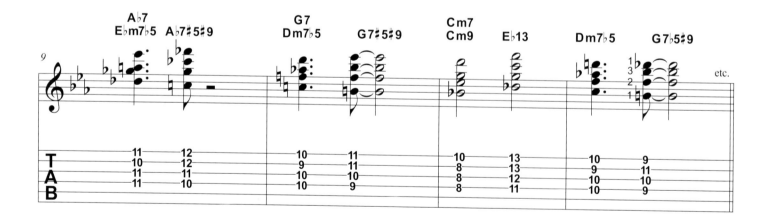

"**Into Somewhere.**" This example puts chord scales to work in a tune you've seen before, first with three-note open-voiced chords and then with walking bass lines. One small difference from the previous two tunes is that here the comp's upper note ventures onto the second string.

Bars 1, 10, 16, and 21 feature new chords with the uppermost voice on the second string, as well as some new harmonies not included in the chord scales presented previously. Again, any given scale tone can be harmonized with more than one voicing.

"Into Somewhere"

Track 12

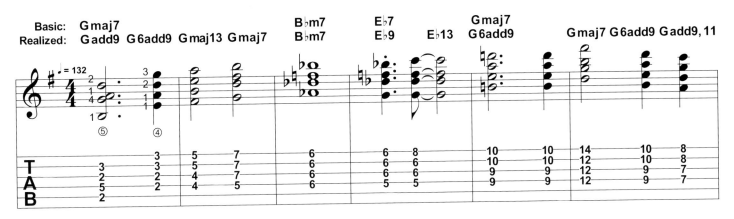

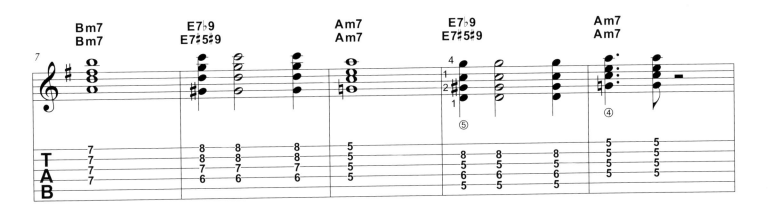

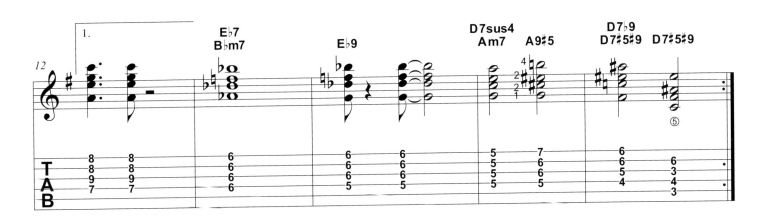

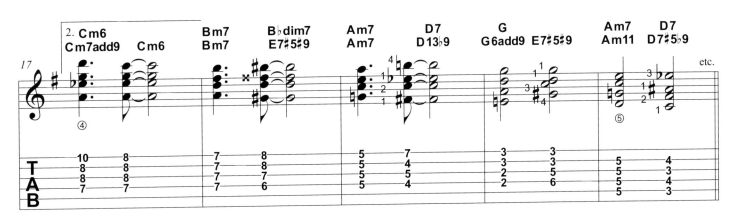

5 COMPING WITH CLOSE-VOICED THREE-NOTE CHORDS

Strictly speaking, the majority of chords in this book are partial in that they omit certain notes, often the root and/or 5th. What distinguishes the harmonies in this chapter is that they contain three notes whose lower and upper notes are an interval less than an octave.

Close-voiced partials often contain the 3rd and 7th (guide tones), with the third note being an extension or alteration. Easy to finger, they enable you to easily avoid playing the root in the bass, and they can give you a degree of flexibility not possible with four-note chords. (Notice the similarity between these chord scales and the lower three notes of the previously discussed four-note chord scales.)

To get started, take a look at the following chord scales, the upper note of which is on the second string. Learn them well, so that you can effortlessly transpose them to other keys. And, as before, be sure to assemble them into IIm-V7-Imaj sequences.

"**Five Minus One**" is an uptempo tune in the key of E♭ major that features some common, easy-to-play three-note IIm7-V7s.

The example commences with a chromatic pickup that leads to E♭maj9. In measures 4 and 5, notice how the upper voice descends chromatically from F to F♭(E) to E♭. The opposite occurs in bars 8 through 10, where the upper voice ascends from E♭ to E to F to F♯. Three-note close-voiced harmonies make it especially easy to create movement among the various voices.

Throughout, there are several rhythmic anticipations. In bar 6, Amaj13 is anticipated, and the end of bar 11 foreshadows B♭7.

Notice the overall 16-bar form. To conclude the tune, honor the fine in measure 19, or play through the next measure to repeat.

"Five Minus One"

Track 13

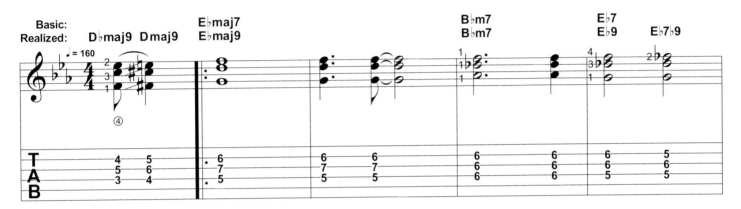

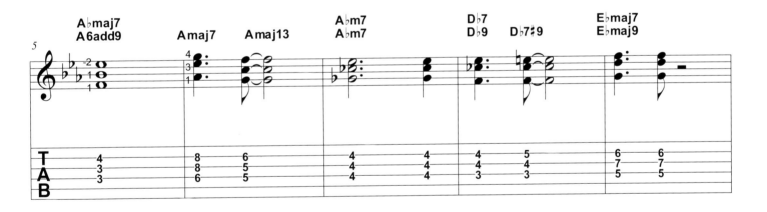

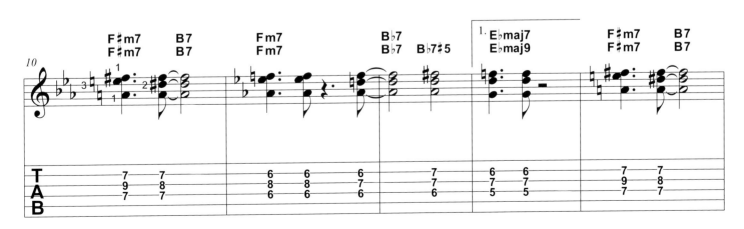

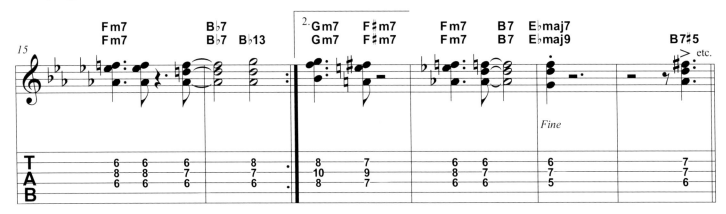

Bossa nova & "**Sea Swell**." Partial chords work great for Latin music. Unlike the previous bossa, this one uses a two-bar rhythmic pattern. Not only that, observe that it anticipates the second measure of the pattern by an eighth value.

Here the song structure is AABA, with the A section being 12-bars long, and the B section being eight. This difference between the A and B sections is not all that common in jazz.

In bars 7 to 9, the basic changes suggest an internal moving line with an Eb-D-Db-C-B descent, although the "realized" changes opt for a more simplified version.

It's good to keep in mind that fake book changes occasionally reflect an elaborate original arrangement of a melody and that players sometimes choose to use a simpler set for improvisational purposes. Alternative changes such as these are occasionally referred to as "blowing changes," although blowing changes can represent an altogether additional section of a tune. (Notice that the bridge utilizes "slash" chords, where the letter to the right of the slash calls for a specific bass note.)

The last two measures of the A section constitute a vamp that both leads back to the A section and into B. It can also be used as an introduction and ending. And while the chart has a fine on the last beat, you can extend the final vamp and then end on a D major chord, such as Dmaj7#11. None of this is in the music shown here, but it does represent how a jazz player might spontaneously treat the tune. The chord progression of the B section represents a common bridge that can be found in other tunes, although, they of course support a different melody in a different key.

Track 14

"Sea Swell"

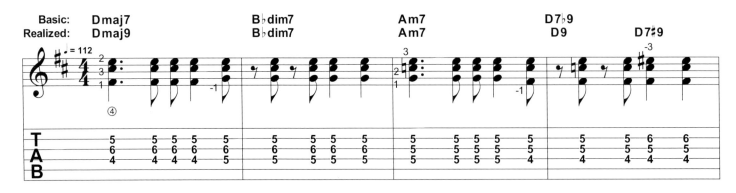

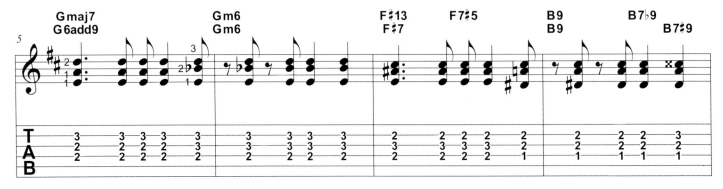

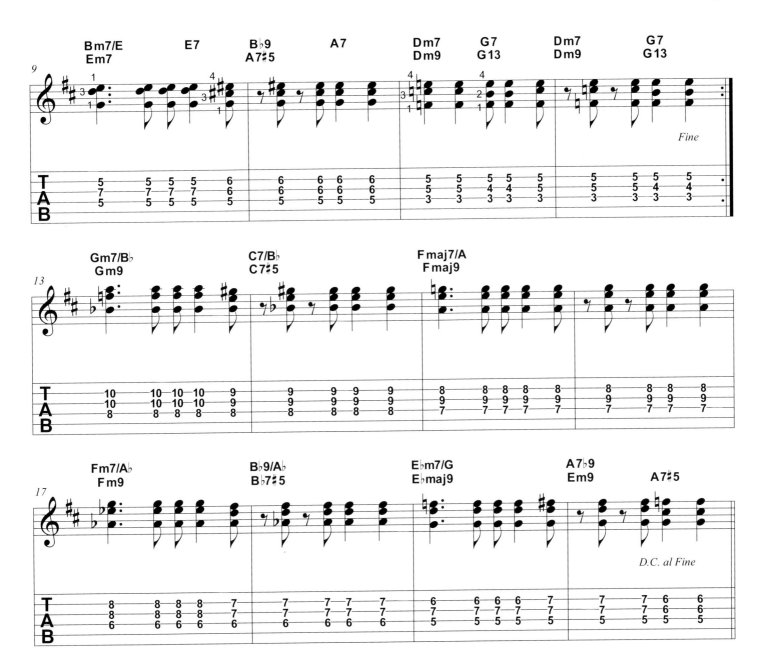

"All The Things You Want" will give your new knowledge of three-note close voicings a real workout, not only because it's in the key of A♭ major (although it begins on VIm7; actually VIm9), but also because it is this book's longest example at 36 bars and arguably its most complex. Before we take a look at its myriad interesting aspects, let's see how its chords progress.

Notice the various series of chords whose roots move counterclockwise through the circle of fifths, including bars 1 through 5, 6 and 7, 9 through 13, 14 and 15, 17 through 19, 21 through 23, 25 through 29, and 33 through 35. Also appreciate the chromatic sequence in measures 30 through 33. Once you've examined these sections, especially note how they are connected, often by a half-step shift up or down.

Three-note chords allow for close connections throughout. The quick rhythmic figures help kick things along, and the transition from a thirdless A♭6add9 to D♭maj9 offers a nice solution to this chord combination.

The fill used in bars 7 through 9 continues the piece's movement, and creates contrary motion in the lower voices as Em7 moves to Cm (B moves down to B♭, as D moves up to E♭). Another major-based fill is used in measures 15 through 17, where Gmaj7 leaps to Cmaj7 and then chromatically descends to Amadd9 in bar 17 (this Amadd9 is an interesting structure; try inverting it, using only the notes in the chord).

Also, notice the differences between the basic and realized changes in bars 30 through 32 where a descending chromatic sequence is turned into a series of IIm7-V7s.

To end the piece, finish with an A♭maj; the IIm7-V7 in bar 36 (here Gm7-C7♯5) takes you back to the top to repeat the form.

"All The Things You Want"

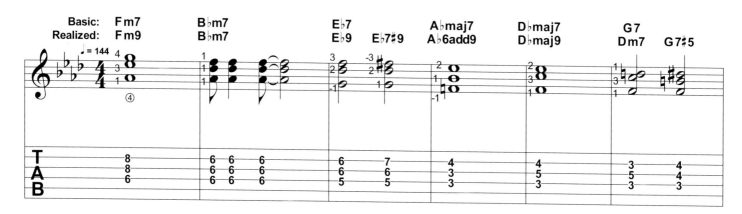

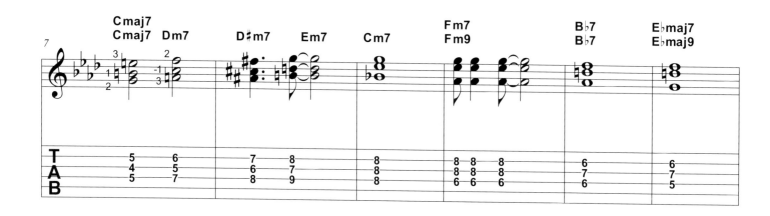

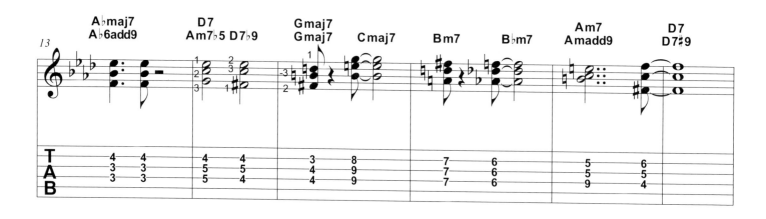

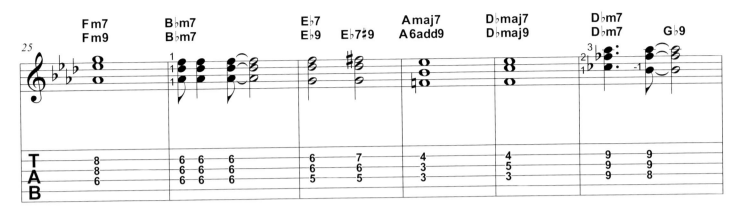

Modal comping. A modal tune is based on a particular mode (often Dorian). Since most modal tunes are harmonically static in that they employ few chords, one way to generate harmonic interest is to modalize the chords by using the chord indicated in the chart as a suggested starting point, and then move the notes up or down through the mode by step, although leaps also can be incorporated. Partial chords greatly simplify this process.

Here are two eight-bar examples. (For the B section, modal tunes often shift up a half-step.) In the first eight measures, a Dm9 partial serves as a starting point, while Dm7 is used for the second eight.

It's important to grasp that when you modalize a chord, you are simultaneously generating new harmonic structures and also exploiting the extensions of the basic chord. Modalization can also be used in comping standards, as mentioned in terms of the minor blues in Chapter 4.

You can also approach modal tunes in a direct manner whereby you play different voicings of the prevailing chord and maybe break up the repetition with half-step approaches; however, taking a modal approach is not only more in the spirit of this type of music, but gives you a wealth of options not possible with direct comping.

That being said, you can also feel free to mix direct and modal approaches with not only the chords shown here, but also ones based on two- and four-note structures, and even chords generated from pentatonic scales and other sources.

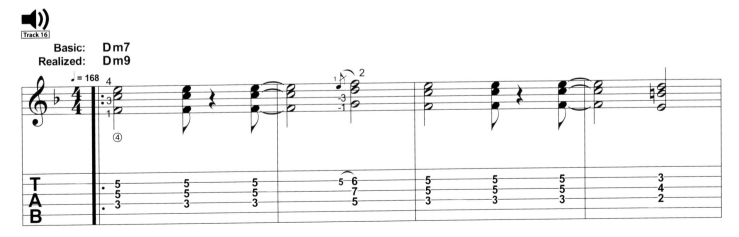

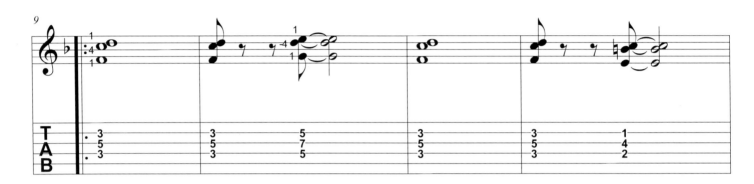

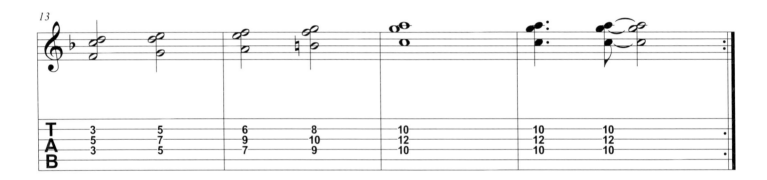

Mixing three- and four-note chords. As mentioned throughout this book, comping is not a rigid process, but one that can accommodate more than one approach, sometimes simultaneously. The following example demonstrates how you can combine four- and three-note voicings and should generally be considered a starting point for your own ideas as your fluency increases.

"Mixetta" is a 32-bar tune in F major whose bridge begins in measure 11 as it moves to A minor (a I major to III minor relationship).

At certain points, some new chords that aren't members of the chord scales presented earlier are utilized (see bars 1, 7, 9, and 15). Again, keep in mind that the upper note of a chord scale can support more than one voicing, and sometimes several.

The first instance of mixed voicings occurs in measures 3 through 8, where several exchanges take place, as if one big band section is countering another. Seen in an earlier example, a particularly hip voicing is shown in bar 7: D7♯5♯9. Again, you may recognize this chord as A♭13. Notice that these spellings are reciprocal ♭5 substitutes.

In bars 12 through 17, the bass chromatically descends from G♯ to G to F♯ to F to E, again illustrating the close connections made possible by three-note voicings.

To complete the tune, return to the top and take the first ending, at which point you'll be beginning a new 32-bar chorus. While there are many ways to end any given tune, the coda shows a variation on a common concluding sequence (that also appears in the body of some numbers, including Cole Porter's "Night And Day" and Vince Guaraldi's "Christmas Time Is Here"). You might find it useful to think of this sequence as beginning on the ♭Vm7♭5 chord (in this case, Bm7♭5).

"Mixetta"

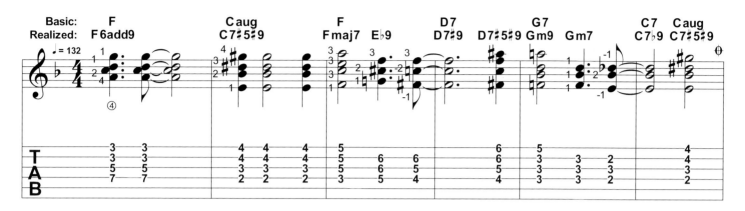

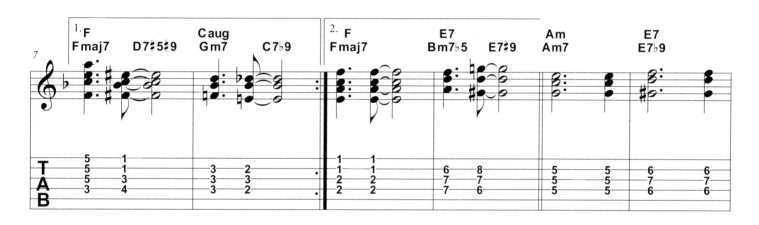

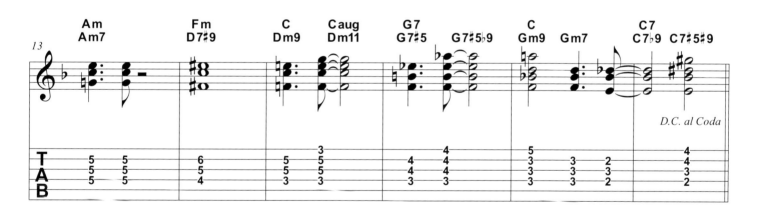

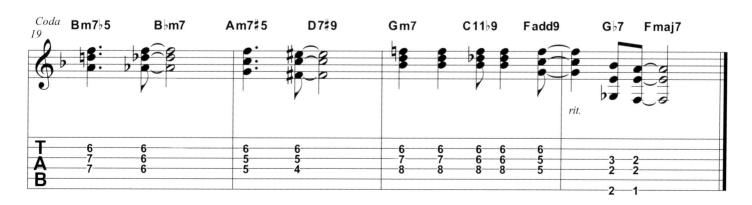

NOTATIONAL SYMBOLS

The following text explains the symbols and notation—common to most guitar music— used in this book.

Tablature. Horizontal lines represent the guitar's strings, the topmost line being the first (high E) string. Numbers designate the frets to be played (for instance, a 2 on the third line means to play the third string, 2nd fret, A). Time values are shown in the standard notation (other symbols are explained in the following text).

General symbols. In the standard notation, left-hand fingering is indicated by small Arabic numerals near the note heads (1 = 1st finger, 2 = 2nd, 3 = 3rd, 4 = pinky).

Circled numbers indicate the string a single note or the lowest note of a chord is to be played on. A circled number applies until the string changes.

Hammer-ons (from a lower note to a higher note) and pull-offs (from higher to lower) are indicated with a tie:

A bent note is shown in parentheses and is connected by a tie to the unbent note. For an upward bend, play the first note and bend up to the pitch in parentheses. For a reverse bend, pre-bend the note to the specified pitch and then release to the indicated note:

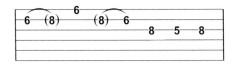

Slides are indicated with a combination of ties and straight lines. For slides between notes (connected by a tie and a straight line), play the first pitch and slide up or down to the next pitch as required. For a slide that approaches a note from no specific point,

quickly slide up to the destination note:

Chord diagrams. Vertical lines represent strings, horizontal lines represent frets. A thick black line represents the nut, an arc indicates a barre, Roman numerals indicate the fret at which a diagram is oriented, Xs stand for strings that are unplayed or muted, open circles are open strings, black dots show finger placement, and small numbers indicate fingering:

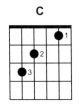 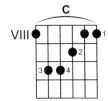

ABOUT THE AUTHOR

Jim Ferguson enjoys a multi-dimensional career as an educator, performer, composer, and author. *Just Jazz Guitar Magazine* describes him as "a wonderful composer and a multi-faceted virtuoso guitar player."

Through his many articles in *Guitar Player Magazine*, where he served as Associate Editor, he shaped how the guitar is viewed and played.

Jim's instructional books, which include *All Blues For Jazz Guitar—Comping Styles, Chords & Grooves* and *All Blues Soloing For Jazz Guitar—Scales, Licks, Concepts & Choruses*, Mel Bay best sellers, have received universal acclaim.

He also has numerous solo classical guitar compositions to his credit. In addition to *Just Jazz Guitar*, his work has been hailed by Great Britain's *Classical Guitar Magazine*, as well as figures such as celebrated conductor JoAnn Falletta.

Jim is profiled in Maurice J. Summerfield's *The Jazz Guitar—Its Evolution, Its Players And Personalities Since 1900*, has contributed numerous entries to the *New Grove Dictionary of Jazz*, and was nominated for a Grammy for annotating Fantasy Records' *Wes Montgomery— The Complete Riverside Recordings.*

Jim received a Master of Fine Arts Degree in music from Mills College in Oakland, California, and went on to teach in California universities and colleges for over two decades. He resides in Santa Cruz, California, where he continues to compose, teach privately, and write.